NUTRITION FOR WEIGHT LOSS SURGERY

Fifty in a Flash

Fresh Food Fast

SALLY JOHNSTON & JUSTINE HAWKE

ACCREDITED PRACTISING DIETIANS | ACCREDITED NUTRITIONISTS

Contents

Introduction 5
Bacon & Egg Breakfast Muffins 7
Coffee Breakfast Shake 7
Eggs in Sauce 9
Smashed Avocado & Feta on Toast 9
Banana Pikelets 11
Baked Pears with Ricotta & Cinnamon 11
Nutty Banana Smoothie 13
Banana, Peach & Vanilla Smoothie 13
Overnight Oats Four Ways 15
Cracker Toppings & Wrap Fillings 17
Cheesy Vegetable Fritters 19
Corn & Chickpea Fritters with Feta & Dill 19
Mediterranean Pizza 21
Sweet Corn, Bean & Feta Salad with Zucchini Ribbons 21
Mexican Salad Cups 23
Chunky Tomato & Bean Soup 23
Vietnamese Chicken Noodle Salad 25
Salmon Poke Bowl 25
Grilled Beef Salad with Pear & Blue Cheese 27
Chicken & Haloumi Salad with Spinach, Strawberries & Asparagus 27
Tuna & Corn Wonton Pies 29
Prawns with Cucumber & Mango Salsa 29
Mushroom & Rocket Mountain Bread Quiche 31
Beef Nacho Bowl 33
Chicken Tacos 33
Hamburgers 35
Grilled Pork with Black Rice Salad 35
Roasted Beetroot & Lentil Salad with Yoghurt & Tahini Dressing 37
Moroccan Spiced Mince 37
Tandoori Lamb Salad 39
Green Chicken Curry 39
Beef Pho 41
Sang Choy Bau Inspired Pork Mince 41
Indian Spiced Lamb with Pappadams 43
Pad Thai 43
Chicken Paella 45
Chilli Lime Fish with Broccolini 45
Tray Baked Lamb & Vegetables 47
Beef & Bean Burritos 47
Chunky Chicken, Zucchini & Capsicum Frittata 49
Italian Style Baked Chicken 49
Asian Inspired Slow Cooked Beef 51
Sweet Chilli Beef Cups 51
Spinach, Tomato & Pine Nut Zucchini 'Pasta' 53
'Cheeseburger' Meatballs 53
Satay Prawn Stir-fry 55
Miso & Ginger Salmon with Baked Vegetables 55

Introduction

Fifty in a Flash, Fresh Food Fast is food that is not only quick and easy to prepare, but is tasty and nutritious, with weight loss surgery goals in mind.

Some points to consider when using this recipe book are detailed below.

SMALL SERVES

Each recipe specifies how many small serves it makes. 'Small serves' refers to a side plate, or bread and butter plate sized serve. In the case of smoothies, it refers to approximately one cup.

However, we know that after weight loss surgery the amount of food that people tolerate varies enormously. Only ever eat to your individual capacity, eating until you are satisfied, never full.

If you want to make a single serve, simply reduce the ingredients. For example, if a recipe says it serves four and you want to only make one serve, then simply use one quarter of each ingredient.

MILK AND MILK PRODUCTS

When selecting yoghurt, milk and cheese, consider your goals. If your priority is to reduce your energy (calorie/kilojoule) intake to lose weight, or if you use dairy products in larger volumes, then reduced fat options may be an appropriate choice for you.

If you are weight stable, looking to gain some weight or use milk products in smaller volumes, then full cream products are typically an appropriate choice.

Reduced fat milk, cheese and yoghurt were used in the recipe analysis throughout this book as this represents an average.

PROTEIN POWDER

When we refer to 'good quality protein powder', our first choice is a whey protein isolate. Whey is the best source of leucine, an amino acid that is important in muscle sparing.

If you don't like the taste of whey, egg white protein powders are also very high quality and are a good alternative as they are rapidly absorbed by the body. If you prefer a plant based powder, look for options based on a pea and rice blend as these contain the best amino acid profiles.

SUITABLE TO FREEZE

Look out for recipes with the above icon as they are suitable to freeze. This generally refers to the protein portion of the meal. Freezing of accompaniments such as noodles, taco shells, bread or salad vegetables is not recommended.

Bacon & Egg Breakfast Muffins

MAKES 3 SMALL SERVES
(2 MUFFINS PER SERVE)

1 teaspoon olive oil
75g shortcut bacon, fat trimmed, diced
1 mushroom, diced
6 eggs
2 tablespoons good quality protein powder
2 tablespoons milk
2 spring onions (white part), thinly sliced
½ tomato, diced
1/8 red capsicum, diced
Small handful baby spinach, shredded
½ cup tasty cheese, grated
Freshly ground black pepper

Preheat oven to 180°C. Line a 6 cup muffin tin with paper liners or spray with cooking spray and set aside. Heat oil in a frying pan, add bacon and mushroom and cook gently for a few minutes, then set aside. In a large bowl, beat eggs. Dissolve protein powder into the milk, not the other way around, and add to beaten eggs. Add cooked bacon, mushrooms and remaining ingredients to the egg mixture and combine. Spoon a ⅓ cup of mixture into each muffin pan. Bake for 20-25 minutes or until the center of the muffin is cooked.

Nutrition information (per 2 muffin serve): kilojoules 975, calories 233, protein 26g, fat 12.5g, saturated fat 5g, carbohydrate 3.5g, fibre 1.5g.

Coffee Breakfast Shake

MAKES 2 SMALL SERVES

1 cup milk
2 tablespoons good quality protein powder
2 short shots of espresso coffee, chilled (or 2 teaspoons instant coffee dissolved in ¼ cup water)
½ cup coffee flavoured gelato
5 ice cubes

Dissolve protein powder in ¼ cup of the milk by mixing the powder into liquid to dissolve it, not the other way round. Place the remaining milk, espresso, gelato and ice in a blender or food processor and blend until well combined. Slowly add the dissolved protein powder and blend on low speed to combine.

Nutrition information (per cup): kilojoules 590, calories 141, protein 11g, fat 4.5g, saturated fat 2.5g, carbohydrate 15g, fibre negligible.

Eggs in Sauce

MAKES 4 SMALL SERVES

1 teaspoon olive oil
1 onion, diced
2 cloves garlic, crushed
2 cups tomato passata or tomato based pasta sauce
8 eggs
Oregano, to taste
Freshly ground black pepper

Heat olive oil in a frying pan. Add onions and garlic and sauté until onions are starting to soften. Add passata or pasta sauce, bring to the boil then reduce heat to a simmer. Whilst sauce is simmering, crack eggs into the sauce and season with oregano and pepper. Allow to cook until the eggs are cooked to your liking.

Nutrition information (per serve): kilojoules 875, calories 209, protein 14g, fat 11g, saturated fat 2.5g, carbohydrate 12.5g, fibre 4.5g.

Smashed Avocado & Feta on Toast

MAKES 4 SMALL SERVES

1 avocado, peeled, stone removed
Squeeze of fresh lemon juice
4 slices grainy bread, toasted
80g feta, crumbled
Freshly ground black pepper

Place avocado in a bowl with a large squeeze of lemon juice and mash roughly until just combined. Spoon one quarter of the avocado mixture onto each of the slices of toast. Top with feta and cracked black pepper to serve.

Nutrition information (per serve): kilojoules 1000, calories 239, protein 9g, fat 15.5g, saturated fat 5g, carbohydrate 13g, fibre 4g.

Banana Pikelets

MAKES 4 SMALL SERVES
(4 MINI PIKELETS PER SERVE)

1 banana, mashed
4 eggs, whisked
1 teaspoon vanilla essence
Cinnamon to taste
2 tablespoons wholemeal self-raising flour
2 tablespoons good quality protein powder
2 teaspoons olive oil
400g Greek yoghurt
1 apple, grated

Combine the first six ingredients together. Heat olive oil in a frying pan. Add small spoons of the mixture into the pan and cook until bubbles appear. Flip and cook the other side. Layer the pikelets with apple and yoghurt to form a mini stack.

Nutrition information (per serve): kilojoules 1010, calories 241, protein 16g, fat 8.5g, saturated fat 3.5g, carbohydrate 22.5g, fibre 4.5g.

Baked Pears with Ricotta & Cinnamon

MAKES 4 SMALL SERVES

2 pears, halved
1½ cups ricotta cheese
2 tablespoons natural peanut butter
1 tablespoon good quality protein powder
½ teaspoon cinnamon

Preheat oven to 180°C. Sit pear halves on a tray (lined with baking paper), skin side down. Bake pears for 30 minutes or until tender. Whilst pears are baking, add ricotta, peanut butter and protein powder to a small bowl and combine. Remove pears from the oven and top with ricotta mixture. Sprinkle with cinnamon to serve.

Nutrition information, per serve: kilojoules 845, calories 202, protein 11g, fat 9.5g, saturated fat 3g, carbohydrate 12g, fibre 4g.

Nutty Banana Smoothie

MAKES 2 SMALL SERVES

2 tablespoons good quality protein powder
1 cup milk
1 banana
1 tablespoon natural peanut butter
Pinch of salt
5 ice cubes

Dissolve protein powder in ¼ cup of the milk by mixing the powder into liquid to dissolve it, not the other way round. Place remaining ingredients in a blender or food processor and blend until well combined. Slowly add the dissolved protein powder and blend on low speed to combine.

Nutrition information (per cup): kilojoules 855, calories 204, protein 12.5g, fat 9g, saturated fat 2.5g, carbohydrate 18g, fibre 2g.

Banana, Peach & Vanilla Smoothie

MAKES 2 SMALL SERVES

2 tablespoons good quality protein powder
¼ cup milk
1 banana, peeled
1 fresh peach or 4 tinned peach quarters, drained
3/4 cup milk
2 tablespoons vanilla yoghurt
5 ice cubes

Dissolve protein powder in ¼ cup milk by mixing the powder into liquid to dissolve it, not the other way round. Roughly chop fruit and place in blender with remaining milk, yoghurt and ice and blend until smooth. Slowly add the dissolved protein powder and blend on low speed to combine.

Nutrition information (per cup): kilojoules 730, calories 174, protein 11g, fat 2.5g, saturated fat 1.5g, carbohydrate 25.5g.

Overnight Oats Four Ways

MAKES 4 SMALL SERVES

½ cup oats
3 tablespoons good quality protein powder
1 grated apple
1 cup milk

½ cup water
1 tablespoon chia seeds
4 tablespoons almond meal
½ teaspoon cinnamon

METHOD FOR ALL OVERNIGHT OATS

Combine all ingredients together and refrigerate overnight. To serve, add your desired toppings, as per the suggestions below.

Berries & Yoghurt

Top each serve with 1 tablespoon of fresh or frozen berries and 1 tablespoon of Greek yoghurt.

Nutrition information, per serve: kilojoules 805, calories 192, protein 10.5g, fat 8g, saturated fat 1.5g, carbohydrate 17g, fibre 5g.

Banana & Walnuts

Top each serve with ¼ banana, sliced and 2 teaspoons of crushed walnuts.

Nutrition information, per serve: kilojoules 965, calories 231, protein 10g, fat 11.5g, saturated fat 1.5g, carbohydrate 19.5g, fibre 5g.

Cranberries & Mixed Seeds

Top each serve with 2 teaspoons of dried cranberries and 2 teaspoons of mixed seeds.

Nutrition information, per serve: kilojoules 925, calories 221, protein 10.5g, fat 10.5g, saturated fat 1.5g, carbohydrate 19g, fibre 5g.

Sultanas & Peanut Butter Yoghurt

Top each serve with 1 teaspoon of sultanas and 1 tablespoon of Greek yoghurt blended with 1 teaspoon of smooth peanut butter.

Nutrition information, per serve: kilojoules 1005, calories 240, protein 12g, fat 11.5g, saturated fat 2g, carbohydrate 20g, fibre 5g.

Cracker Toppings & Wrap Fillings

For the following cracker toppings and wrap fillings, place all ingredients in a bowl and mix until well combined. They can be stored in the fridge for up to three days and can be served in a grainy wrap, lettuce leaf, on top of grainy crackers, on a halved sandwich thin as an open sandwich or as a 'dip' with vegetable sticks.

Classic Tuna

MAKES 6 X1/4 CUP SERVES

185g can of tuna in spring water, drained
1 gherkin, finely diced
Squeeze of fresh lemon juice
1 tablespoon dill, chopped

2 stalks celery, strings removed and finely diced
¼ red onion, finely diced
2 teaspoons wholegrain mustard
2 tablespoons mayonnaise

Nutrition information (per1/4 cup serve): kilojoules 320, calories 76, protein 5g, fat 5.5g, saturated fat 1g, carbohydrate 1g, fibre 0.5g.

Chilli Tuna & Roasted Capsicum

MAKES 8 X1/4 CUP SERVES

185g can chilli tuna in oil, drained
¼ cup chargrilled capsicum, diced

1 cup cottage cheese

Nutrition information (per1/4 cup serve): kilojoules 330, calories 78, protein 8.5g, fat 4.5g, saturated fat 1.5g, carbohydrate 0.5g, fibre negligible.

Egg, Chive & Mayo with Radish

MAKES 8 X1/4 CUP SERVES

6 hard boiled eggs, peeled and roughly chopped
1 tablespoon mayonnaise
1 radish, finely diced
Pinch of salt

1 stalk celery, strings removed and finely diced
2 tablespoons Greek yoghurt
1 tablespoons chives, chopped
Freshly ground black pepper

Nutrition information (per1/4 cup serve): kilojoules 275, calories 66, protein 4.5g, fat 5g, saturated fat 1g, carbohydrate 1g, fibre 0.5g.

Waldorf Inspired Chicken Salad

MAKES 4 X1/4 CUP SERVES

100g cooked chicken breast, shredded or finely diced
1 stalk celery, finely diced
1 tablespoon Greek yoghurt

½ apple, finely diced
4 walnuts, crushed
1 tablespoon mayonnaise

Nutrition information (per1/4 cup serve): kilojoules 440, calories 105, protein 8g, fat 6.5g, saturated fat 1g, carbohydrate 3g, fibre 1g.

Cheesy Vegetable Fritters (F)

MAKES 4 SMALL SERVES
(2 FRITTERS PER SERVE)

2 cups grated or diced vegetables as desired e.g. carrot, onion, corn, zucchini, capsicum, baby spinach.
3 eggs
1 cup grated tasty cheese
¼ cup spelt (or wholemeal) flour
1 tablespoon olive oil

Place all ingredients except oil in a bowl and mix well to combine. Heat the oil in a frying pan and add heaped tablespoons of the mixture to the pan. Cook until golden on both sides. Repeat until all mixture is used.

Nutrition information (per 2 fritter serve): kilojoules 850, calories 203, protein 15g, fat 12.5g, saturated fat 5g, carbohydrate 7.5g, fibre 2g.

Corn & Chickpea Fritters with Feta & Dill (F)

MAKES 4 SMALL SERVES
(2 FRITTERS PER SERVE)

125g can corn kernels, drained
125g can chickpeas, drained and 'smashed'
1 small zucchini, grated
Small handful of baby spinach, chopped
80g feta, crumbled
2-3 sprigs of dill, chopped finely
1 egg
1/3 cup besan (chickpea flour)
1 tablespoon olive oil

Place all ingredients except oil in a bowl and mix well to combine. Heat oil in a frying pan and add heaped tablespoons of the mixture to the pan. Cook until golden on both sides. Repeat until all mixture is used.

Nutrition information (per 2 fritter serve): kilojoules 795, calories 190, protein 9g, fat 11g, saturated fat 4g, carbohydrate 11.5g, fibre 3g.

Mediterranean Pizza

MAKES 4 SMALL SERVES

4 small pita pockets
2 tablespoons relish
80g mozzarella cheese, grated
80g feta cheese, crumbled
1 tomato, sliced
2 pickled artichoke hearts, sliced
¼ cup chargrilled red peppers sliced
6 kalamata olives, sliced

Preheat oven to 180°C on grill setting. Spread each pita with relish and top with cheeses, tomato and pickled vegetables. Place under grill and cook until cheese is melted and golden.

Nutrition information (per pizza): kilojoules 1035, calories 248, protein 11.5g, fat 12.5g, saturated fat 6.5g, carbohydrate 20g, fibre 4g.

Sweet Corn, Bean & Feta Salad with Zucchini Ribbons

MAKES 4 SMALL SERVES

2 tablespoons Italian white vinegar
1 tablespoon olive oil
1 teaspoon Dijon mustard
Fresh thyme to taste
½ cup sweet corn kernels, drained
1 cup four bean mix, drained
Handful of green beans, sliced
1 small zucchini, peeled into ribbons using a potato peeler
½ green capsicum, diced
80g feta cheese, crumbled

To make dressing, combine vinegar, oil, mustard and thyme in a jar and shake well to combine. Add all other ingredients to a bowl and stir. Add dressing to serve.

Nutrition information (per serve): kilojoules 765, calories 182, protein 8.5g, fat 9.5g, saturated fat 3.5g, carbohydrate 12g, fibre 5g.

Mexican Salad Cups

MAKES 4 SMALL SERVES

400g can four bean mix, drained and rinsed
400g sweet corn kernels
1 tomato, diced
1 small green capsicum, diced
½ avocado, diced
Handful of fresh mint, shredded
Handful of fresh coriander, shredded
4 lettuce leaf cups
Juice of one lime
Fresh chilli to taste

Add beans, corn, salad vegetables, avocado and herbs to a bowl and stir to combine. Divide bean mixture between lettuce cups. Squeeze over fresh lime and top with chilli to taste.

Nutrition information (per cup): kilojoules 748, calories 179, protein 7.5g, fat 5.5g, saturated fat 1g, carbohydrate 20.5g, fibre 8g.

Chunky Tomato & Bean Soup (F)

MAKES 4 SMALL SERVES

2 teaspoons olive oil
1 brown onion, finely diced
2 cloves garlic, crushed
400g diced canned tomatoes
1 cup salt reduced vegetable stock
2 cans Mexican Beans (or four bean mix)

Heat oil in a frying pan. Add onions and garlic and sauté until onion softens. Add tomatoes, stock and beans and bring to the boil. Reduce heat and simmer for five minutes. Note that this soup can be simmered for an extra 10 minutes to evaporate some of the liquid and make a tomato and bean 'stew'.

Nutrition information (per serve): kilojoules 770, calories 184, protein 9.5g, fat 3.5g, saturated fat 0.5g, carbohydrate 22g, fibre 10.5g.

Vietnamese Chicken Noodle Salad

MAKES 4 SMALL SERVES

50g dry rice noodles
1 cup chicken stock
200g chicken breast
1 cup Chinese cabbage, finely sliced
1 carrot, cut into match sticks
1 small red capsicum, finely sliced
Handful fresh mint
1 tablespoon rice vinegar
Juice of ½ a lime (cut other half in wedges to serve)
1 tablespoon fish sauce (or to taste)
1 clove garlic, crushed
1 teaspoon sriracha (chilli sauce)
1 teaspoon palm or brown sugar (optional)
Fresh chilli and lime wedges to serve

Cook rice noodles according to instructions on packet. Set aside. Bring stock to a simmer. Poach chicken in stock until cooked through, remove from stock and using two forks, pull apart until shredded. Place noodles, cabbage, carrot, capsicum and mint in a bowl and top with shredded chicken. To make dressing, combine the next six ingredients in a small jar and shake well. Pour dressing over salad and top with chilli and lime wedges to serve.

Nutrition information (per serve): kilojoules 675, calories 161, protein 16.5g, fat 2.5g, saturated fat 0.5g, carbohydrate 16.5g, fibre 3.5g.

Salmon Poke Bowl

MAKES 4 SMALL SERVES

1 1/3 cups cooked brown rice
240g smoked or cooked salmon, sliced
1 carrot, cut into match sticks
1 Lebanese cucumber, halved, deseeded and sliced
2 spring onions, finely sliced
Pickled ginger to taste
½ avocado, cubed
1 tablespoon soy sauce
2 tablespoons rice vinegar
1 clove garlic crushed
1 teaspoon honey (if desired)

Divide brown rice between four bowls. Top with salmon, vegetables, pickled ginger and avocado. Combine soy, vinegar, garlic and honey in a small jar and shake well. Pour over bowls to serve.

Nutrition information (per serve): kilojoules 1160, calories 279, protein 16g, fat 13g, saturated fat 2.5g, carbohydrate 22g, fibre 3.5g.

Grilled Beef Salad with Pear & Blue Cheese

MAKES 4 SMALL SERVES

Large handful of rocket
50g blue cheese, crumbled
1 pear, thinly sliced
40g pecans
300g lean beef fillet, grilled or barbequed
1 teaspoon Dijon mustard
2 tablespoons Italian white vinegar
1 tablespoon olive oil
1 teaspoon honey (if desired)

Combine rocket, cheese, pears and pecans. Slice cooked beef fillet thinly and place over salad. To make dressing, combine mustard, vinegar, oil and honey in a small jar and shake well. Pour over salad to serve.

Nutrition information (per serve): kilojoules 1260, calories 367, protein 21g, fat 20g, saturated fat 5g, carbohydrate 7g, fibre 3g.

Chicken & Haloumi Salad with Spinach, Strawberries & Asparagus

MAKES 4 SMALL SERVES

Large handful of baby spinach leaves
8 strawberries, quartered
8 asparagus spears, trimmed and blanched
½ avocado, diced
200g chicken tenderloins, grilled
160g haloumi, sliced and grilled
1 tablespoon balsamic vinegar
1 tablespoon olive oil

Combine baby spinach, strawberries, blanched asparagus, and avocado. Top with grilled chicken and haloumi. Combine balsamic vinegar and olive oil and pour over salad to serve.

Nutrition information (per serve): kilojoules 1140, calories 272, protein 25g, fat 17g, saturated fat 6.5g, carbohydrate 3g, fibre 2.5g.

Tuna & Corn Wonton Pies (F)

MAKES 4 SMALL SERVES
(2 WONTON PIES PER SERVE)

8 fresh wonton wrappers
185g tuna in spring water, drained
1 egg
4 tablespoons Parmesan cheese
1 cup smooth ricotta cheese
2 tablespoons corn kernels

Preheat oven to 180°C. Place wonton wrappers into muffin trays. Combine tuna, egg, Parmesan, ricotta and corn in a bowl. Divide mixture evenly between wonton wrappers and bake for 15-20 minutes or until set and golden.

Nutrition information (per serve): kilojoules 980, calories 234, protein 22g, fat 9.5g, saturated fat 5.5g, carbohydrate 13.5g, fibre 0.5g.

Prawns with Cucumber & Mango Salsa

MAKES 4 SMALL SERVES

50g dry rice noodles
24 green king prawns, peeled and deveined
Juice of ½ lemon
1 tablespoon soy sauce
½ teaspoon sesame oil
1 Lebanese cucumber, deseeded and sliced
1 small mango, diced
1 small red capsicum, finely sliced
1 small red chilli sliced (or to taste)
1 handful fresh mint, chopped
1 handful fresh coriander, chopped
Juice of ½ a lemon

Cook rice noodles according to instructions on packet. Set aside. To marinade prawns, combine lemon juice, soy sauce and sesame oil and pour over the prawns. Set aside. To make cucumber and mango salsa, combine cucumber, mango, capsicum, chilli and herbs, and squeeze over remaining lemon juice. Season to taste. Set aside. Barbeque or pan fry prawns for 1-2 minutes each side until cooked. Divide cooked noodles between four bowls, place prawns on top of noodles then spoon over the Cucumber & Mango Salsa.

Nutrition information (per serve): kilojoules 875, calories 209, protein 26.5g, fat 1.5g, saturated fat negligible, carbohydrate 20g, fibre 3g.

Mushroom & Rocket Mountain Bread Quiche ⓕ

MAKES 4 SMALL SERVES

Oil spray
2 slices of mountain bread*
200g mushrooms
1 teaspoon olive oil
2 cloves of garlic, crushed
Handful of rocket, roughly chopped
2 spring onions, finely chopped
½ cup smooth ricotta
½ cup milk
6 eggs, lightly beaten
2 tablespoons Parmesan cheese, finely grated
Freshly ground black pepper

Pre-heat oven to 180°C. Spray a ceramic quiche or pie dish with oil spray. Place one piece of mountain bread in the bottom. Brush the second slice of mountain bread with a little egg and (egg side down) turn the square to a diamond position and place on the first mountain bread, so it appears like a star.

Heat oil in a frying pan and cook the mushroom and garlic until the mushrooms have softened. Add the rocket and spring onion and cook for another minute then remove from the heat. Spoon this mixture over the mountain bread lined dish. Spoon dollops of the ricotta over the top of the mushroom mixture.

Combine milk, beaten eggs and Parmesan cheese and whisk together. Pour this over the mushroom mixture. Grind some black pepper over the top and bake in the oven for 25-30 minutes or until browned and just set. (You may find that the egg runs under the mountain bread but this is fine).

Remove from the oven and stand for 10 minutes before serving. Cut into quarters and serve with a small side salad if desired. Can be served hot or cold.

Nutrition Information (per serve): kilojoules 795kJ, calories 190, protein 16.5g, fat 9g, saturated fat 3.5g, carbohydrate 9g, fibre 2.5g.

* To help you select the best wraps or mountain breads, check out our Weight Loss Surgery Shopping Companion available via our online store at www.nfwls.com

Beef Nacho Bowl

MAKES 4 SMALL SERVES

1 teaspoon olive oil
½ onion, grated
300g lean beef mince
1 teaspoon taco seasoning
4 tablespoons salsa
1 tomato, diced
½ red capsicum, diced
Baby cos lettuce, shredded
½ avocado, diced
2/3 cup grated tasty cheese
4 tablespoons Greek Yoghurt

Heat oil in a frying pan. Add onion and sauté until it softens. Add mince and brown. Add taco seasoning and salsa to mince and cook through. Divide mince between four bowls. Add tomato, capsicum, lettuce, avocado and cheese to bowls. Top each with a tablespoon of yoghurt to serve.

Nutrition information (per serve): kilojoules 1185, calories 283, protein 25g, fat 16g, saturated fat 6.5g, carbohydrate 8g, fibre 3g.

Chicken Tacos

MAKES 4 SMALL SERVES

1 teaspoon olive oil
1 onion, diced
400g chicken mince
1 cup salsa
400g can kidney beans, drained and rinsed
4 taco shells
1 carrot, grated
1 tomato, diced
Lettuce, finely shredded, to serve

Heat oil in a frying pan. Add onion and cook until softened. Add chicken and cook until browned. Add salsa and beans to chicken and stir to warm through. Add mince mixture to tacos and top with carrot, tomato and lettuce.

Nutrition information (per serve): kilojoules 1310, calories 313, protein 26g, fat 10g, saturated fat 3g, carbohydrate 24g.

Hamburgers (F)

MAKES 4 SMALL SERVES (1 PATTY PER SERVE)

½ carrot, grated
½ zucchini, grated
250g lean mince
1 egg
½ cup kidney beans, mashed
1 tablespoon BBQ or tomato sauce
Dash of Worcestershire sauce (optional)
1 teaspoon olive oil
1 onion, finely sliced
1 slice wholegrain bread per person to serve (optional)
BBQ or tomato sauce, to serve
4 slices reduced fat cheese
1 tomato
4 lettuce leaves

Place grated carrot and zucchini on a clean tea towel. Roll up tea towel and wring out any excess moisture. Combine mince, egg, kidney beans, zucchini, carrot and sauce in a mixing bowl and mix well. Shape mixture into four patties. Heat olive oil in a frying pan. Add onion and cook until softened. Remove from pan and set aside. Add the mince patties to the frying pan and brown each side for approximately five minutes each side or until cooked through. Toast bread (if using) and top with patties, sauce, onion rings, cheese and salad.

Nutrition information (per serve, without bread): kilojoules 975, calories 233, protein 24.5g, fat 8g, saturated fat 3.5g, carbohydrate 13g, fibre 4g.

Grilled Pork with Black Rice Salad

MAKES 4 SMALL SERVES

1 cup cooked black rice
½ red capsicum, diced
½ yellow capsicum, diced
Handful of fresh mint, shredded
½ red onion, finely diced
¼ cup slivered almonds
1 tablespoon seeds
2 tablespoons currants
1 tablespoon olive oil
Juice of 1 lemon
300g pork fillet, grilled
4 tablespoons Greek yoghurt

Combine rice, capsicum, mint, red onion, almonds, seeds and currants.

To make dressing, combine olive oil and lemon juice in a small jar and shake well. Drizzle salad with dressing. Thinly slice pork fillet and add to salad. Top with a tablespoon of Greek yoghurt per serve.

Nutrition information (per cup): kilojoules 1160, calories 278, protein 24g, fat 12g, saturated fat 2g, carbohydrate 16.5g, fibre 4g.

Roasted Beetroot & Lentil Salad with Yoghurt & Tahini Dressing

MAKES 4 SMALL SERVES

4 beetroot, peeled and cubed
1 tablespoon olive oil
200g Greek yoghurt
Juice of half a lemon
1 teaspoon tahini
1 teaspoon honey
400g can brown lentils, drained
1 cup mixed fresh herbs e.g. parsley, mint and tarragon
2 tablespoons macadamias

Preheat oven to 180°C. Drizzle beetroot with olive oil and roast in the oven approximately 20 minutes, until soft. Whilst beetroot is roasting, prepare the dressing by combining yoghurt, lemon juice, tahini and honey in a small bowl or jug and mixing well. Combine cooked beetroot, lentils, herbs and macadamias in a bowl and drizzle with yoghurt dressing to serve.

Nutrition information (per serve): kilojoules 1115, calories 266, protein 12g, fat 11.5g, saturated fat 2.2g, carbohydrate 24.5g, fibre 8.5g.

Moroccan Spiced Mince

MAKES 8 SMALL SERVES

2 teaspoons olive oil
1 brown onion, diced
2 garlic cloves, crushed
500g lean lamb or beef mince
2 - 3 teaspoons Moroccan seasoning
1 tomato, diced
1 carrot, sliced into strips using a potato peeler
2 stalks celery, strings removed, thinly sliced or diced
1 zucchini, grated
¼ cup currants
3 tablespoons lemon juice
½ cup salt reduced chicken stock
400g can chickpeas, drained
2 tablespoons pine nuts, toasted
2 tablespoons fresh flat leaf parsley, chopped
4 tablespoons Greek yoghurt, to serve
Pita bread, to serve (optional)

Heat oil in a frying pan over medium heat. Add onion and garlic and cook for 3 to 4 minutes or until softened. Increase heat and add mince. Cook, stirring to break up mince, until browned. Add Moroccan seasoning and cook, stirring, for a minute or until fragrant. Add tomato, carrot, celery, zucchini, currants, lemon juice and stock. Bring to the boil. Reduce heat to low and simmer for 10 minutes or until thickened. Stir through the chickpeas, pine nuts and parsley. Serve garnished with parsley and 1 tablespoon of natural yoghurt. Serve with flatbread if desired.

Nutrition information (per serve, without bread): kilojoules 915, calories 218, protein 18g, fat 10.5g, saturated fat 3g, carbohydrate 11g, fibre 4g.

Tandoori Lamb Salad

MAKES 4 SMALL SERVES

2 tablespoons tandoori paste
1 tablespoon Greek yoghurt
300g lamb loin (back strap)
2 tablespoons Italian white vinegar
1 small red onion, thinly sliced
2 small handfuls baby spinach
1 Lebanese cucumber, halved, deseeded and thinly sliced
1 handful fresh mint, shredded
1 handful fresh coriander, shredded
Fresh sliced chilli to taste
2 small wholemeal pita pockets, toasted and cut into wedges
1 tablespoon mango chutney
200g Greek yoghurt
Juice of half a lemon

Combine tandoori paste and yoghurt. Coat lamb with yoghurt mixture and set aside to marinate for at least 15 minutes. Pour vinegar over sliced onion, season with a little salt and pepper and set aside. Cook lamb to your liking on the barbeque or grill. Remove from heat and let rest for a few minutes. Thinly slice. Remove onion from vinegar. Combine spinach, cucumber, herbs, pickled onion, chilli and pita. To make dressing, combine last three ingredients in a small jar and shake well. Top salad with lamb and dressing to serve.

Nutrition information (per serve): kilojoules 1135, calories 271, protein 29g, fat 7.5g, saturated fat 2.5g, carbohydrate 18.5g, fibre 5.5g.

Green Chicken Curry (F)

MAKES 4 SMALL SERVES

1 teaspoon olive oil
400g chicken, trimmed of fat, cut into strips eg. breast, thigh or tenderloin
2½ tablespoons green curry paste
2/3 cup Carnation Light & Creamy evaporated milk, coconut flavor (or plain evaporated milk with a tiny drop of coconut essence)
1 tablespoon fish sauce
1 tablespoon Kaffir lime leaves, shredded
1 cup baby corn
1 cup green beans, trimmed, sliced diagonally
1 small red capsicum, sliced
2 teaspoons cornflour

Heat olive oil in a frying pan. Add chicken and stir-fry for 5 minutes or until starting to brown. Add curry paste and stir fry until fragrant. Stir in evaporated milk, fish sauce and kaffir lime leaves and bring to the boil. Reduce heat to low, add corn, green beans and capsicum and simmer until tender. Whilst simmering, dissolve cornflour in just enough water to make a paste. Add to the simmering curry, stirring until well combined. This should help thicken the sauce.

Nutrition information (per cup): energy 880kJ, calories 211, protein 26.5g, fat 5.5g, saturated fat 1.5g, carbohydrate 10.5g, fibre 4g.

Beef Pho

MAKES 4 SMALL SERVES

50g dry rice noodles
4 cups beef stock
1 small piece ginger, grated
1 onion, sliced
3 cloves garlic
4 star anise
200g beef eye fillet, thinly sliced
4 button mushrooms, thinly sliced
1 handful bean sprouts
1 handful herbs eg. mint, coriander, basil
Fresh red chilli, sliced, to taste

Cook rice noodles according to instructions on packet. Set aside. Place stock, ginger, onion, garlic and star anise in a pot, bring to the boil then reduce heat and simmer for 15 minutes. Remove from heat and drain stock to remove solids. Return drained stock to the pot and warm. Add sliced beef, mushrooms and rice noodles to the stock and allow beef to cook through. Divide soup between four bowls and top with bean sprouts, herbs and chilli to taste.

Nutrition information (per serve): kilojoules 578, calories 138, protein 14g, fat 3.5g, saturated fat 1g, carbohydrate 11.5g, fibre 2.5g.

Sang Choy Bau Inspired Pork Mince (F)

MAKES 4 SMALL SERVES

2 teaspoons olive oil
2 garlic cloves, crushed
2 teaspoons minced ginger
400g lean pork mince (chicken, turkey or beef mince can be used if you prefer)
3 spring onions, thinly sliced
2 tablespoons oyster sauce
1 tablespoon soy sauce
1 tablespoon kecap manis (sweet soy sauce)
½ teaspoon sesame oil
2 teaspoons lime juice
1 carrot, grated
225g can water chestnuts, drained, chopped
Lettuce leaf cups, to serve
Handful fresh coriander, to serve
2 tablespoons peanuts, roasted and chopped

Heat olive oil in a wok over medium to high heat. Add garlic and ginger and cook for a minute or two until fragrant. Add mince and stir-fry for about 5 minutes, or until browned, breaking up mince as it cooks. Add spring onions, sauces, sesame oil and lime juice and stir-fry until well combined. Add carrot and water chestnuts and stir-fry for 1 to 2 minutes until carrot is tender. Spoon mixture into lettuce leaf cups and top with fresh coriander and peanuts. Note mince mixture can be frozen.

Nutrition information (per serve): kilojoules 1210, calories 289, protein 22.5g, fat 16.5g, saturated fat 5g, carbohydrate 11g, fibre 3.5g.

Indian Spiced Lamb with Pappadams (F)

MAKES 4 SMALL SERVES

1 teaspoon olive oil
400g lamb, trimmed of fat, diced
1 onion, diced
1 clove garlic, crushed
Small fresh red chilli, finely diced
½ tablespoon grated fresh ginger
1 teaspoon cumin seeds
1 handful fresh or ½ teaspoon ground coriander
½ teaspoon turmeric
400g can chopped tomatoes
1 cup sweet potato, diced
½ cup cooked chickpeas (or canned chickpeas, drained and rinsed)
8 mini microwavable pappadams
4 tablespoons Greek yoghurt

Pre-heat oven to 150°C. Heat oil in a frying pan. Add lamb and brown on both sides. Transfer to a baking or casserole dish. Return the frying pan to the heat and add onion, cook until onion is golden in colour. Add the garlic, chilli, ginger and spices and cook for 1-3 minutes or until fragrant then pour in the tomatoes. Stir until combined, reduce to a simmer and simmer for about 10 minutes or until the sauce has reduced a little. Meanwhile scatter the diced sweet potato and chickpeas over the lamb. When the sauce has reduced a little, pour over the lamb, sweet potato and chickpeas. Cover and bake in the oven for ¾ hour or until the lamb has cooked through and the sweet potato is tender. Arrange pappadams around the edge of the microwave plate. Microwave on high for approximately 60 seconds or until they are crisp. Divide the lamb and sauce evenly amongst the bowls, and serve with pappadams and a tablespoon of yoghurt.

Nutrition Information (per serve): kilojoules 1225kJ, calories 293, protein 29g, fat 8.5g, saturated fat 2.5g, carbohydrate 21g, fibre 7.5g.

Pad Thai

MAKES 4 SMALL SERVES

1 tablespoon peanut oil
2 eggs, lightly beaten
4 spring onions, thinly sliced
1 small carrot, cut into matchsticks
½ red capsicum, thinly sliced
2 garlic cloves, crushed
1 small red chilli, seeds removed, finely chopped
250g green prawns
2 tablespoons soy sauce
Juice of 1 lime
2 teaspoons brown sugar
1 cup rice stick (Pad Thai) noodles, cooked
2 tablespoons peanuts
Handful coriander leaves, to serve
Lime wedges, to serve

Heat a wok over high heat. Add about one third of the oil and swirl to coat the pan. Pour egg into the wok and cook over medium heat, tilting the wok until almost set. Remove omelet from the wok, roll tightly, slice thinly and set aside. Add another third of the oil to the wok and swirl to coat the pan. Add the spring onions, carrot and capsicum and stir-fry for 3-4 minutes, so the vegetables are tender crisp. Remove from the wok and set aside with the egg. Add the final third of the oil to the pan then add the garlic, chilli and prawns. Stir-fry for 3-5 minutes or until the prawns are just pink. Combine soy sauce, lime juice and sugar. Return, omelet and vegetables to the wok, add the noodles and sauces and stir-fry until all ingredients are well combined. Spoon onto plates and top with peanuts and coriander. Serve with lime wedges.

Nutrition information (per serve): kilojoules 1080, calories 258, protein 20g, fat 10g, saturated fat 2g, carbohydrate 20.5g, fibre 3.5g.

Chicken Paella

MAKES 4 SMALL SERVES

1 teaspoon olive oil
1 red onion, thinly sliced
3 garlic cloves, crushed
400g chicken mince
2 tomatoes, chopped
½ red capsicum, sliced
½ zucchini, halved and sliced
¼ cup rice
¾ cup salt reduced chicken stock
½ teaspoon saffron threads
2 teaspoons paprika
Chilli flakes, to taste
½ cup frozen peas
Freshly ground black pepper

Heat oil in a frying pan or wok over medium-high heat. Add onion and garlic and cook for 3 to 4 minutes or until starting to soften. Add chicken mince and cook, stirring to break up the mince, for 5 minutes. Add tomatoes, capsicum and zucchini and cook for 2 minutes. Stir in rice, stock, saffron, paprika and chilli if desired. Stir well to combine and bring to the boil. Cover and reduce heat to low. Simmer for 15 to 20 minutes or until the stock is absorbed. Stir in peas until heated through. Season with pepper to serve.

Nutrition information (per serve): kilojoules 1060, calories 253, protein 23.5g, fat 8g, saturated fat 2g, carbohydrate 19g, fibre 5g.

Chilli Lime Fish with Broccolini

MAKES 4 SMALL SERVES

2 tablespoons sweet chilli sauce
2 tablespoons lime juice
1 tablespoon rice vinegar
1 tablespoon finely chopped lemon grass
1 clove garlic, crushed
4 x 120g firm fish fillets eg. salmon, barramundi, flathead,
1 teaspoon peanut oil
4 spring onions, sliced diagonally
½ red capsicum, thinly sliced
1 bunch broccolini

Preheat oven to 180°C. Line an oven tray with baking paper. Combine sweet chilli sauce, lime juice, rice vinegar, lemongrass and garlic in a bowl. Add fish and turn to coat. Place fish on baking paper and spoon over a little of the marinade. Bake for around 10-12 minutes then let stand for 5 minutes. Whilst fish is baking, heat peanut oil in a pan and stir fry spring onions, capsicum and broccolini until just tender. Serve fish with stir fried vegetables.

Nutrition information (per serve): kilojoules 800, calories 191, protein 26.5g, fat 3.5g, saturated fat 0.5g, carbohydrate 11g, fibre 3g.

Tray Baked Lamb & Vegetables

MAKES 4 SMALL SERVES

4 baby potatoes, quartered (optional)
2 tablespoons of olive oil
½ red capsicum, cut into strips
½ green capsicum, cut into strips
1 red onion, cut into wedges
8 cherry tomatoes or 2 large tomatoes, quartered
Handful of fresh oregano and rosemary, chopped
400g lean lamb eg. backstrap, fillet
Juice and zest of one lemon
1 teaspoon Dijon mustard
2 cloves crushed garlic
½ teaspoon dried oregano

Preheat oven to 180°C. Place potatoes on a baking tray and drizzle with 1 tablespoon of the olive oil. Bake for 20 minutes. Remove tray from oven and add vegetables, herbs and lamb. Combine lemon juice, zest, 1 tablespoon of oil, mustard, garlic and dried herbs in a jar and shake to combine. Pour over lamb and vegetables and return tray to oven. Bake for a further 20-30 minutes until cooked to your liking.

Nutrition information (per serve): kilojoules 1360, calories 325, protein 26.5g, fat 15.5g, saturated fat 3.5g, carbohydrate 17g, fibre 5.5g.

Beef & Bean Burritos

MAKES 8 SMALL SERVES

1 teaspoon olive oil
1 onion, finely chopped
1 garlic clove, crushed
300g lean beef mince
1 teaspoon ground cumin
1 teaspoon smoked paprika
¼ teaspoon chilli powder
1 can chopped tinned tomatoes
½ red capsicum, chopped
1 tablespoon tomato paste
½ cup salt reduced beef stock
125g can kidney beans, drained and rinsed
1 handful coriander leaves, chopped
8 wholegrain wraps e.g. tortillas or mountain bread*
½ cup reduced fat tasty cheese, grated
½ avocado, diced
4 tablespoons Greek yoghurt

Heat oil in a frying pan. Add onion and garlic and cook for 5 minutes or until onion is tender. Add mince and cook, stirring, for 3 minutes or until mince is browned. Add cumin, paprika and chilli powder and cook, stirring, for about 1 minute, or until fragrant. Add tomatoes, capsicum, tomato paste and stock. Bring to the boil. Reduce heat to low and simmer, uncovered, for 10 minutes or until sauce is thickened. Stir in the beans and coriander. Spread beef mixture along the centre of tortillas and sprinkle with cheese, avocado and yoghurt. Roll up to enclose filling.

Nutrition information (per serve): kilojoules 1005, calories 240, protein 17g, fat 8.5g, saturated fat 3.5g, carbohydrate 20g, fibre 5g.

* To help you select the best wraps or mountain breads, check out our Weight Loss Surgery Shopping Companion available via our online store at www.nfwls.com

Chunky Chicken, Zucchini & Capsicum Frittata (F)

MAKES 4 SMALL SERVES

1 teaspoon olive oil
250g chicken, trimmed of fat, diced into cubes eg. breast, thigh or tenderloins
1 zucchini, halved and sliced
1 red capsicum, sliced
5 eggs
1 teaspoon dried mixed herbs or 1 handful fresh mixed herbs
¼ cup reduced fat grated cheese

Preheat oven to 180°C. Line a cake tin or baking dish with baking paper. Heat oil in a frying pan. Add the chicken, zucchini and capsicum and cook for approximately 5 minutes or until tender. Remove from heat and spread over the base of the tin or dish. Combine eggs, herbs and cheese in a jug and whisk to combine. Pour over the chicken and vegetables. Bake in the oven for 20-25 minutes or until firm and golden.

Nutrition Information (per serve): energy 830kJ, calories 199, protein 24.5g, fat 9g, saturated fat 3g, carbohydrate 4g, fibre 2g.

Italian Style Baked Chicken (F)

MAKES 4 SMALL SERVES

400g chicken e.g. breast, thigh or tenderloin
425g can diced tomatoes
170g jar artichokes, drained
1 red onion, sliced
4 mushrooms, sliced
¼ cup chargrilled capsicums, sliced
½ cup dry pasta shapes e.g. fusilli, macaroni, shells
Freshly ground black pepper

Preheat oven to 180°C. Place all ingredients in a baking dish and combine. Cook in oven at 180°C for 30 minutes or until chicken is cooked through.

Nutrition information (per serve): kilojoules 900, calories 215, protein 27, fat 3.5g, saturated fat 1g, carbohydrate 15g, fibre 5g.

Asian Inspired Slow Cooked Beef ⓕ

MAKES 4 SMALL SERVES

500g beef, diced
2 stalks celery, sliced
½ cup salt reduced beef stock
¼ cup salt reduced soy sauce
1 tablespoon brown sugar
2 teaspoons sesame oil
2 garlic cloves, crushed
1 tablespoon cornflour
1 head broccoli, cut into small florets
1 red capsicum
1/3 cup brown rice

Add beef and celery to a slow cooker. In a small bowl combine beef stock, soy sauce, sugar, oil and garlic. Add to the slow cooker and stir well. Cook on high for approximately 8 hours. In the last half hour prior to serving, remove 2-4 tablespoons of the cooking liquid from the slow cooker and mix with cornflour to make a paste, add to the slow cooker. Steam or stir fry capsicum and broccoli to your liking and add to the slow cooker. Stir well to combine. Cook for another half an hour or until the sauce thickens. If the sauce is not thickening, remove the lid. Meanwhile, cook rice according to directions on the packet. Serve rice with slow cooked beef.

Whilst the cooking process takes hours, the preparation can be done quickly and left to cook over the day, hence meeting our 'fresh food fast' approach.

Nutrition information (per cup): energy 1270kJ, calories 304, protein 32g, fat 9g, saturated fat 2.5g, carbohydrate 21g, fibre 3.5g.

Sweet Chilli Beef Cups

MAKES 4 SMALL SERVES

1 teaspoon peanut oil
1 onion, diced
400g lean beef mince
2 tablespoons sweet chilli sauce
2 tablespoons hoisin sauce
1 carrot, grated
1 cup cabbage, shredded very finely
4 iceberg lettuce leaf cups

Heat oil in a wok over medium to high heat. Add onion and cook until softened. Add mince and stir-fry for about 5 minutes, or until browned. Add sauces and stir-fry until well combined. Add carrot and cabbage and stir-fry for 1 to 2 minutes until carrot is tender. Spoon mixture into lettuce leaf cups to serve.

Nutrition Information (per serve): kilojoules 1100kJ, calories 263, protein 24g, fat 11g, saturated fat 4g, carbohydrate 16g, fibre 4.5g.

Spinach, Tomato & Pine Nut Zucchini 'Pasta'

MAKES 4 SMALL SERVES

130g tub Philadelphia Protein Extra Light Cream Cheese
425g can crushed tomatoes
2 cloves garlic, crushed
¼ cup sundried tomatoes, sliced
¼ cup seeded black olives, sliced
100g baby spinach
2 medium zucchinis, spiralized into noodles
¼ cup pine nuts, toasted
4 tablespoons parmesan cheese

Combine cream cheese, undrained tomatoes and garlic in pan. Bring to a simmer and simmer for a few minutes, uncovered, until sauce starts to thicken. Add sundried tomatoes and olives and combine well. Add spinach and mix through until wilted. Add zucchini noodles and pine nuts and mix through until the mixture is heated through. Sprinkle with parmesan cheese to serve.

Nutrition information: kilojoules 815, calories 195, protein 8.5g, fat 12g, saturated fat 1.5g, carbohydrate 10.5g, fibre 5.5g.

'Cheeseburger' Meatballs (F)

MAKES 10 SMALL SERVES
(PER 2 MEATBALLS OR 1 PATTY PER SERVE)

500g lean beef mince
1 cup multigrain breadcrumbs
2 tablespoons tomato relish
1 tablespoon mild American mustard
2 eggs
Lettuce, to serve
Sliced cheese, to serve
Sliced tomato, to serve
Pickles, to serve

Place mince, breadcrumbs, relish, mustard and eggs in a bowl and mix well. Roll into walnut sized balls or small patties. Place onto a non-stick or oiled oven tray and place in a pre-heated oven at 180°C for 15-20 minutes or until cooked through and golden. Serve with lettuce, cheese, tomato and pickles.

Nutrition information (per 2 meatballs or 1 patty with tomato, lettuce, cheese and pickles): kilojoules 1020, calories 244, protein 21g, fat 11g, saturated fat 5.5g, carbohydrate 14.5g, fibre 1.5g.

Satay Prawn Stir-fry

MAKES 4 SMALL SERVES

50g dry rice noodles
¼ cup natural crunchy peanut butter
¼ cup Carnation Light & Creamy evaporated milk, coconut flavor (or plain evaporated milk with a tiny drop of coconut essence)
2 teaspoons oyster sauce
1 tablespoon sweet chilli sauce
2 teaspoons soy sauce
2 teaspoons peanut oil
400g green prawns
½ red onion, cut into wedges
2 garlic cloves, crushed
1 cup snow peas, sliced
1 red capsicum, thinly sliced

Cook rice noodles according to instructions on packet. Set aside. To make sauce, combine the first five ingredients in a jug and set aside. Heat wok over high heat with 1 teaspoon of oil. Add prawns and stir-fry for a minute until the prawns turn pink. Remove prawns and set aside. Reheat the wok over high heat and add remaining oil. Add onion and garlic and stir-fry for 2 minutes. Add the snow peas and capsicum and stir-fry for 1 minute. Return the prawns to the wok, pour over satay sauce and stir-fry for 2 minutes or until the sauce just comes to the boil. Add the cooked noodles and stir until heated through.

Nutrition information (per cup): kilojoules 1450kJ, calories 346, protein 29.5g, fat 14g, saturated fat 2.5g, carbohydrate 22g, fibre 4.5g.

Miso & Ginger Salmon with Baked Vegetables

MAKES 2 SMALL SERVES

1 tablespoon white miso paste
1 tablespoon mirin
1 tablespoon soy sauce
1 teaspoon fresh ginger, grated
240g skinless Atlantic salmon, cubed
½ eggplant, cut into cubes
¼ cauliflower, cut into small pieces
½ red or yellow capsicum, sliced
Small handful coriander, chopped

Combine miso, mirin, soy sauce and ginger to make a marinade. Place salmon cubes and eggplant into marinade and set aside for at least one hour. Preheat oven to 180°C. Line a baking tray with baking paper and place cauliflower, capsicum and marinated eggplant onto the tray and bake in the oven for 15 minutes. Remove tray from the oven, turn all vegetables and place the marinated salmon cubes onto the tray. Return to the oven for 10 minutes, or until salmon is cooked through. Divide baked vegetables between two plates and top with the salmon, sprinkle over coriander and serve.

Nutrition information: kilojoules 1475, calories 352, protein 30g, fat 18g, saturated fat 3.5g, carbohydrate 13g, fibre 6g.

The information in this book is intended for use as a general reference. It is provided on the understanding that it is intended to motivate and educate but is not a replacement for professional advice. It does not constitute advice of a health care professional on any specific health issue/condition. For specific advice tailored to your individual needs consult your surgical team. The authors accept no responsibility for any failure to seek or follow the advice of a healthcare professional and will not be liable for such failure. We only promote products we truly believe are in the interest of our clients.

Nutrition information for recipes is approximate and may vary according to actual ingredients used. Recipes were analysed using Foodworks 9 Professional Edition.

All rights reserved. No part of this publication may be reproduced, stored in a retrieval system or transmitted in any form or by any means, electronic, mechanical, photocopying, recording or otherwise, without the prior written permission of the author. The moral rights of the author have been asserted.

Copyright © Nutrition for Weight Loss Surgery 2019

Recipe Development: Justine Hawke, Sally Johnston and Carmel Cantone.
Food Styling and Photography: Alexandra Gow.
Graphic Design: Jayne Freeman.
Edited by Sally Johnston and Justine Hawke.

www.nfwls.com

www.ingramcontent.com/pod-product-compliance
Lightning Source LLC
Chambersburg PA
CBHW061815290426
44110CB00026B/2878